DOODLE ART ALLEY BOOKS
COLORING BOOK • VOLUME 3

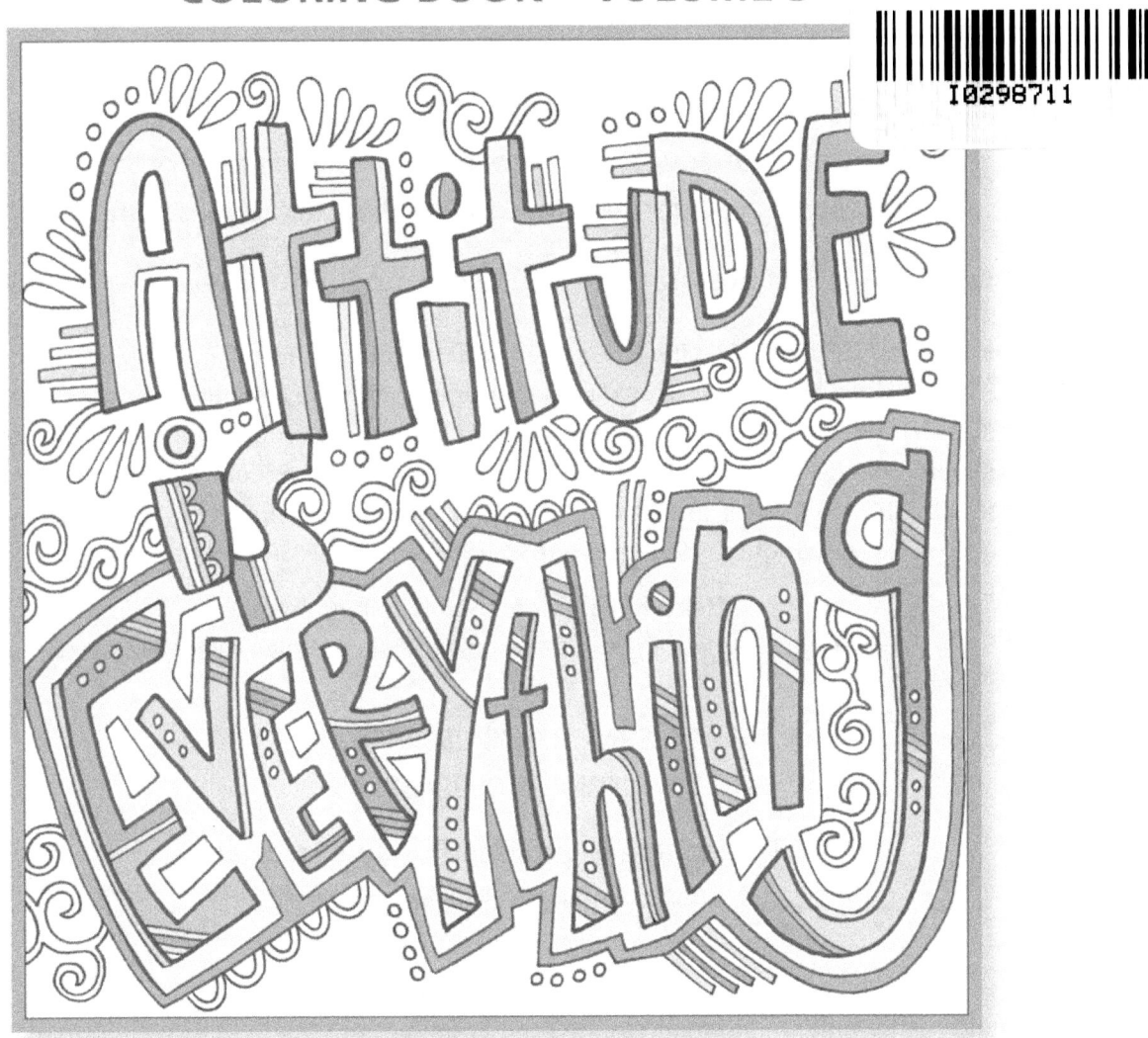

Samantha Snyder

To my dad

Copyright © 2015 Doodle Art Alley.
All rights reserved.

Attitude Is Everything is available at special discounts when purchased in quantities for educational use, fundraising, or sales promotions. For more information, contact: info@akabooks.com

Cover images © 2015 by Doodle Art Alley.

"I dwell in possibility" J 657/F 466 – Line 1 reprinted with permission from THE POEMS OF EMILY DICKINSON: VARIORUM EDITION, edited by Ralph W. Franklin, Cambridge, Mass.: The Belknap Press of Harvard University Press, Copyright © 1998 by the President and Fellows of Harvard College. Copyright © 1951, 1955 by the President and Fellows of Harvard College. Copyright © renewed 1979, 1983 by the President and Fellows of Harvard College. Copyright © 1914, 1918, 1919, 1924, 1929, 1930, 1932, 1935, 1937, 1942 by Martha Dickinson Bianchi. Copyright © 1952, 1957, 1958, 1963, 1965 by Mary L. Hampson.

Helen Keller quote used with permission.
Copyright © American Foundation for the Blind, Helen Keller Archives.

ISBN-13: 978-0692469743
ISBN-10: 0692469745

This edition is published by aka Associates.
www.akabooks.com

Doodle Art Alley Books

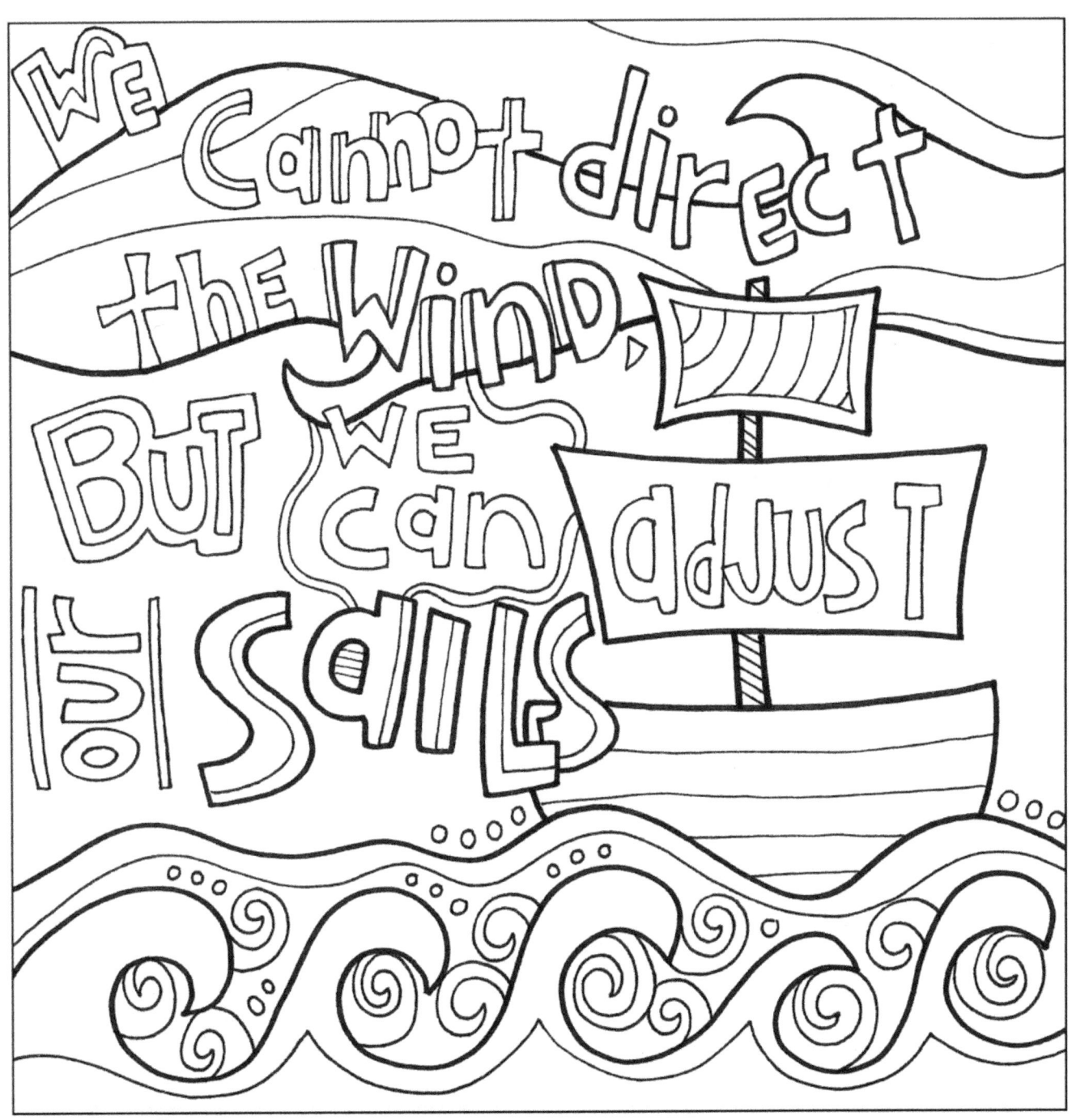

ABOUT DOODLE ART ALLEY

Samantha Snyder has been doodling her whole life. While teaching elementary school, she often drew up coloring pages and printables for her students and fellow teachers. She decided to start sharing her creations and in 2008, Doodle Art Alley was founded.

A quick glance at a doodle may show scribbles, random lines and shapes with no meaning or significance. However, with a little love and direction, these drawings have the potential to compete with some of the best artwork there is!

Doodle Art Alley is dedicated to giving those squiggly lines the proper credit they deserve. Who would have thought that such a small and simple idea could possess so much potential?

There are lots of fun doodle art activities, tips, and information to read through and enjoy. Visit www.doodle-art-alley.com for hundreds of exciting doodles.

Doodle Art Alley Books

www.ingramcontent.com/pod-product-compliance
Lightning Source LLC
Chambersburg PA
CBHW082244300426
44110CB00036B/2436